# DANIEL BOONE'S
## GREAT ESCAPE

MICHAEL P. SPRADLIN          ILLUSTRATED BY ARD HOYT

Walker & Company
New York

**S**nowflakes licked at Daniel Boone's face as he crept quietly alone through the woods. He was hunting—the thing he most loved to do. He didn't know that on this cold and snowy day his life would change forever.

In February 1778, while the Revolutionary War raged back east, Daniel Boone led a party of men to the Licking River in Kentucky to make salt. On the frontier, salt was more valuable than gold because it was needed to preserve meat for the winter. Today he was hunting for food to bring the salt makers.

Boone shot a buffalo, tied several hundred pounds of the meat to his horse, and began the long walk back to the camp. Suddenly the woods went still and quiet in the heavy snowfall. Sensing danger, Boone looked behind him and saw a fearsome sight. Four Shawnee warriors were riding through the trees toward him.

Thinking fast, Boone quickly tried to untie the meat from his horse so he could ride away, but the ropes had frozen solid. He had neglected to clean his knife, and it was now frozen to his scabbard. He was trapped.

Boone sprinted through the trees as the warriors rode after him. The thick snow made it difficult to run. He heard gunfire, and the snow exploded beside him as the rifle shots narrowly missed him. The next shot shattered his powder horn, and Boone knew he must surrender.

The warriors took away Boone's rifle and horse and led him to their war chief, Blackfish. He explained to Boone that the settlers in Kentucky had broken many treaties with the Shawnee. When Chief Cornstalk had visited Fort Randolph under a truce flag to discuss the broken treaties, he had been brutally murdered. The Shawnee felt they had no choice but to attack the Kentucky forts and drive out the settlers.

Boone understood why the Shawnee were angry, but he did not want to fight them. He pleaded with Blackfish to spare his men and said he would convince them to surrender peacefully if Blackfish promised them no harm. He would then lead his men to the Shawnee villages and live with the Shawnee as brothers. In the spring he would go with Blackfish to Boonesborough and convince the settlers there to give up without a fight. After much discussion with his warriors, who still wanted to avenge Cornstalk's murder, Blackfish agreed. Boone led the war party to the camp and persuaded his men to lay down their arms.

On the long march back to Ohio, Blackfish told Boone that while he had promised not to mistreat Boone's men, he had made no such promise to Boone himself. Boone would need to prove his bravery by running the gauntlet. The warriors lined up, facing each other, holding their war clubs. Boone ran quickly through the gauntlet, moving back and forth close to the warriors so they could not easily strike him, struggling to stay on his feet. Near the end of the gauntlet, a warrior jumped in front of Boone and raised his war club with a ferocious cry. Boone lowered his shoulder and knocked the warrior to the ground, reaching the end of the line safely.

When Boone and his men arrived at the Shawnee town of Old Chillicothe, many of them were adopted into the tribe. Boone became the adopted son of Blackfish. He was taken to a river near the village and led into the water. There, the Shawnee women scrubbed his skin with small pebbles and sand to wash away his white blood, making Boone a Shawnee citizen. They named him "Sheltowee," which means "Big Turtle."

Weeks stretched into months. Boone enjoyed his life with the Shawnee. He was allowed to hunt with the young men, village life was calm and peaceful, and the people were kind to him. But Boone knew that the peace would not continue if the Shawnee attacked Kentucky. He understood why the Shawnee felt threatened by the white settlers. But to save his family, he would need to escape.

Boone began to plan for a time when he could slip away to warn the settlements. While hunting, he hid gunpowder in the pockets of his shirt. He would purposely miss targets, hitting a tree instead, returning later to dig out the lead bullet and save it for his escape.

He helped the Shawnee repair their broken guns, hiding the usable pieces of damaged rifles around the village. These parts could be made into a working gun when it was time for him to escape. When everything was ready, Boone watched and waited.

He noticed that large parties of warriors began gathering in Old Chillicothe. Boone listened while the warriors reminded their chiefs of Cornstalk's murder. The warriors wanted vengeance. Blackfish and his men could leave at any moment to attack Kentucky. It was time for Boone to leave.

On June 16, 1778, before the sun came up, Boone slipped out of his *wegiwa*. He moved through the village like a ghost, gathering his makeshift gun and powder, then headed for the safety of the woods. Once there, Daniel Boone began to run.

Boone knew that he had a difficult task ahead of him. When the Shawnee discovered he had escaped, dozens of warriors would come after him. Boonesborough was several days distant, and if he failed, his family and friends would perish.

Soon Boone heard the shouts of the pursuing Shawnee. He ran faster. As the first party of warriors drew nearer, Boone scampered up a tree and hid in the leaves as the Shawnee passed below him. Waiting until they had gone, he climbed down and kept running.

Boone knew that the Shawnee could move through the forest like smoke, making no sound, and he used every trick he knew to avoid capture: he waded through streams to hide his tracks and ran along fallen trees to leave no trail. Whenever the Shawnee came close, he hid in the grass or brush, keeping as still as a statue until they moved on.

Boone kept running through the day and night. His body ached and his feet were sore, but still he ran. When he was too tired to run he stopped to rest, but only for a few moments as the forest was alive with Shawnee.

On the third day, he tied together the parts of his gun and shot a buffalo. While he rested and ate, he crushed bark from an oak tree to make a lotion for his sore feet. He could not rest long, since the Shawnee might have heard the rifle shot. Quickly finishing his meal, he began running again.

Finally Boone reached the wide Ohio River. Crossing it would be the most dangerous part of his journey because he would be captured easily if spotted. He studied the riverbanks carefully and saw the tracks of many horses. He knew that warriors were close by. Still, there was no time to waste.

Cautiously and quietly, Boone pulled a small log from the woods and crept into the water. He tied his gun and powder to the top of the log and held on to it while he floated across the river. The current was strong, and Boone struggled against it as he swam. Nearing the opposite shore he paused, his eyes searching the riverbank for signs of the Shawnee. Seeing no one, Boone quickly paddled to shore, gathered his things, and ran.

And ran.  And ran.

After four solid days of running, Boone finally reached Boonesborough. Since he was dressed like a Shawnee to fool his pursuers, Boone ran to a clearing near the fort and shouted a hello. The gates of the fort swung open, and Boone fell into the arms of his daughter Jemima and his grandchildren, who joyously welcomed him home. His wife, Rebecca, had left Boonesborough and returned to her home back east, because she believed he had been killed by the Shawnee. She would happily rejoin Boone as soon as she was able to make the journey, which took a few months.

Boone was tired. His feet were bloody and his body ached. An attack was coming, but the fort would be safe. All because Daniel Boone ran.

# Epilogue

Boonesborough, founded by Boone when he first entered Kentucky, was an important settlement on the western frontier of the thirteen colonies during the Revolutionary War. After Boone escaped from Old Chillicothe, Blackfish and his warriors attacked the fort. Blackfish asked to meet under a truce flag, and when Boone agreed, Blackfish asked him why he ran away. Boone replied that he missed his family too much. He told Blackfish that he admired him greatly and had received nothing but kindness and respect as a captive. He hoped that his people and the Shawnee could live together in peace. But it was not to be.

During the truce, Blackfish and his men attempted to recapture Boone. Fighting broke out, but Boone made it safely back to the fort. The Shawnee continued the siege of Boonesborough for several days, but Boone's warning had given the settlers time to prepare the fort's defenses. With no chance of victory, the Shawnee returned to the Ohio country. Boone had saved the settlement once again.

Daniel Boone's escape is a stunning act of courage and stamina. His journey from Old Chillicothe, Ohio, back to Boonesborough, Kentucky, through enemy territory—with no weapon other than several pieces of broken rifles that he pieced together—is reduced to one brief sentence in his autobiography, *The Adventures of Daniel Boone:* "On the 16th, before sunrise, I departed in the most secret manner and arrived at Boonesborough on the 20th, after a journey of one hundred and sixty miles, during which I had but one meal."

While a Shawnee captive, Boone was taken to Detroit, where many of the salt makers were ransomed to the British garrison housed there during the Revolutionary War. Boone also managed to convince the British commander not to attack Kentucky, promising that the settlers would surrender in the spring. Boone led him to believe that they would swear allegiance to the British crown, a deception on Boone's part, to buy time so the fort could be warned and defended. Boone's rivals in Kentucky found his quick surrender to the Shawnee and his dealings with the British suspicious. As an officer in the militia, he was court-martialed on charges of treason and collaboration with the enemy. He was found not guilty on all counts.

Kentucky entered statehood in 1792, but by then Boone had long left it behind (feeling it had grown "too full of people"), eventually settling in the Missouri territory. At age seventy-eight, he attempted to join the United States Army to fight against the British in the War of 1812. His request was denied. He died in Missouri on September 26, 1820—about one month shy of his eighty-sixth birthday—after a life full of adventure and exciting exploits, but perhaps none more daring than his great escape.

To my sisters, Regina and Connie,
who took me to the library —M. P. S.

To my brother Brandon, who never passes on a
good adventure —A. H.

Text copyright © 2008 by Michael P. Spradlin
Illustrations copyright © 2008 by Ard Hoyt

First published in the United States of America in 2008 by
Walker Publishing Company, Inc.
Distributed to the trade by Macmillan

For information about permission to reproduce selections from this book, write
to Permissions, Walker & Company, 175 Fifth Avenue, New York, NY 10010

Library of Congress Cataloging-in-Publication Data
Spradlin, Michael P.
Daniel Boone's great escape / by Michael P. Spradlin ; illustrated by Ard Hoyt.
        p.      cm.
ISBN-13: 978-0-8027-9581-6 • ISBN-10: 0-8027-9581-1 (hardcover)
ISBN-13: 978-0-8027-9582-3 • ISBN-10: 0-8027-9582-X (reinforced)
1. Boone, Daniel, 1734–1820—Captivity, 1778—Juvenile literature.
2. Escapes—Kentucky—History—18th century—Juvenile literature. 3. Indian
captivities—Kentucky—History—18th century—Juvenile literature. 4. Shawnee
Indians—History—18th century—Juvenile literature. 5. Frontier and pioneer
life—Kentucky—Juvenile literature. 6. Pioneers—Kentucky—Biography—
Juvenile literature. 7. Explorers—Kentucky—Biography—Juvenile literature. 8.
Kentucky—History—To 1792—Juvenile literature. I. Hoyt, Ard, ill. II. Title.
F454.B66S68 2008     976.9'02092—dc22  [B]     2007050382

Book design by Daniel Roode
Typeset in ACaslon
Art created with watercolor, colored pencil, and pen and ink on Arches paper

Visit Walker & Company's Web site at www.walkeryoungreaders.com

Printed in China
1 2 3 4 5 6 7 8 9 10 (hardcover)
1 2 3 4 5 6 7 8 9 10 (reinforced)

AR

RL    5.6
Pts   0.5